No Weapons

Dawnn Mitchell

American Literary Press, Inc.
Five Star Special Edition
Baltimore, Maryland

No Weapons

Library of Congress
Cataloging in Publication Data
ISBN 1-56167-797-3

Library of Congress Card Catalog Number:
2003090992

Published by

American Literary Press, Inc.
Five Star Special Edition
8019 Belair Road, Suite 10
Baltimore, Maryland 21236

Manufactured in the United States of America

This book of prayers and poetic praises is dedicated in loving memory to my grandmothers, Nina and Mattie and my mother, Michele

ACKNOWLEDGMENTS

All glory and praises go to my Heavenly Father, who sacrificed His only begotten, firstborn, Son for me, a sinner. Father I thank You for this gift and for granting me the courage to openly share it with others.

Thanks to my uncle, Michael Mitchell, whom I know has always loved and cared for me, and the rest of my family for their continued love and support.

Thanks to my spiritual Godmother, Babs Phillips, who loves me like one of her own. Thank you for your guidance, your wisdom, the example of your daily walk with God and your continued love and support.

Thank you, Deborah Oresegun, my spiritual sister, for your continued love, support, guidance and wisdom. I so appreciate you in general, but also for taking and making the time out of your busy schedule to read and assist with the editing of the first draft of this book.

Thank you, Wendy Y. Bailey for sharing your wisdom and for your dedicated time and effort with the first draft also.

And, thank you, Rachel Beck for planting the seed that blossomed into the birth of this book!

I love you all!

Bless those reading this right now, Lord. Caress them with Your
mighty hands Father.

Where healing of any kind is needed, touch them right now with the
healing that comes from the one and only true God, whether it is
finances,
illness,
depression,
diseases,
addiction,
missing a loved one after their home going,
anger with a mate, family member or friend,
loss of a job,
strength in dealing with spiritual wickedness

or whatever it may be, touch them right now Father.

**Please also grant them discernment of demonic spirits, courage to
cast out demons and all demonic spirits, wisdom to know and listen
to Your voice, serenity to accept Your will and the patience to hold
on until the coming of the Lord.**

In the ubiquitous, unchanging, matchless, magnificent, paramount,
eminent name of Jesus Christ I pray! Amen!

FORWARD

This book was written as if to follow a process. As is the case for a builder to construct a house or other building or structure, there must first be a solid foundation. Although the reader is not expected to read this book like a novel, indeed it was written to flow with a beginning, a middle and an 'end', like a novel.

The flow of the beginning reflects the first step toward salvation. This is where we are to accept Jesus Christ as our Lord and Savior, believing He died on the cross and was raised from the dead for our iniquities. And, we are to admit that we are sinners. For some, this is viewed as submission. Some of us may not feel secure in this position because we are forced to realize who is actually in control and how much control we do not have.

There are many self help books, step programs and licensed professionals who, in order to help guide individuals in to becoming more responsible human beings who are able to better cope during trying experiences without resorting to drastic or self-destructive measures, use these same steps toward a new beginning. Indeed, we must accept the fact that we are not in control, admit that we have a problem and submit ourselves to a higher authority. So, there we have it. Acceptance. Admittance. Submission. These are three very vulnerable and bare positions to take in life.

The middle is filled with steps geared toward the cleansing and building of a stronger, more Godly individual. For some of us these are very difficult steps because they are a life long process that forces us to take hard, honest looks at ourselves; at times, this is very difficult to face. All too often these steps are doses of reality we do not want to face or believe. But we must in order to be the clay in God's hands.

Finally, the "end" is filled with the basic ethic of saying thank you, that many of us learn as children. We should be grateful when someone opens or holds a door open for us—they do not have to. It is not their obligation. We should be more than grateful that God chose to save us, to enlighten us with His mercy and His grace—He did not have to. Indeed, He is not obligated to do anything for us!

Dawnn Mitchell, July 16, 2002

TABLE OF CONTENTS

Have mercy on me, O God, have mercy!
I look to You for protection.

-Psalm 57:1 (NLT)

Accepting Christ as Savior   *Inspired by Romans Chapter 10*

Heavenly Father, I humbly come to You right now for a healing that only You can provide. My heart is heavily burdened and I realize that I cannot do this by myself. I realize that I need You more and more each day. I lay all of these burdens down at the altar and ask You to handle them in my stead. I know now that I need You in my life Lord.

I openly confess that I am a sinner,

believing Jesus Christ died on the cross for my sins

and was raised from the dead with all power,

to mend my severed bond with the Sovereign Father.

I openly confess that I accept Jesus Christ as my Lord

and as my Savior.

Lord I want You as my intercessor to plead my case to the Sovereign Father of us all.

Jesus, I know that I need You in every aspect of my life. Indeed, Lord, I want You to be the fence that surrounds me all day and every day.

I want You to be the shield that protects me from all of my enemies. Please place Your helmet on the heads of my enemies to block the evil spirits from penetrating their thoughts, thereby provoking them to cause harm toward me.

Please touch the hearts of my enemies, Father and give them the opportunity to make a conscious decision whether or not to accept the Living Word, my Shepherd, my Lord, my Savior, my Jesus Christ. Father, if they choose to continue to reject Him, please have mercy on them in the name of Jesus Christ. They definitely cannot know what they are doing or what they are giving up. **And Father, please forgive me for every sin I have ever committed. In the name of Jesus Christ I ask these things. Amen**

Prayer for unsaved loved one

Father, I stand in proxy for my loved one who doesn't know Your divine love, who hasn't experienced the joy, peace and freedom of Your will and who doesn't know Your sweet, Holy Spirit.

Although my loved one is not wicked and doesn't cause pain on others deliberately, they are a lost soul and are easy pickings for the enemy of the Lord, without You.

I bind every evil spirit that comes against my loved one. No weapons formed against them shall prosper. I plead the blood of Jesus Christ upon every demonic spirit that is blocking the thoughts of my loved one from making a clear and conscious decision.

Right now they are confused, Father, just as I was before knowing and accepting You.

Touch the heart of my loved one, Lord, so they can know what it is like to feel Your spirit, if only for a moment.

Make them aware of Your presence.

Give them the chance to know what they have been missing in their lives. As You know, we don't know what we have until after it is gone.

Father, please reach my loved one.

I pray for them to experience Your love as I do. Indeed, they are in a place I once was before I accepted Jesus Christ as my Lord and Savior.

Please show them the way, Father.

I know that You love them
even more than I do,
and more than anyone ever will.

I ask in the Precious name of Jesus Christ. Amen.

Prayer in proxy for others   *Inspired by Psalm 10*

Heavenly Father, I humbly come to You now in prayer for those
who don't know You,
who retaliate against all their enemies,
whose mouths are full of cursing, lies and threats,
who have trouble and evil on the tips of their tongues and do not hold
     them or pray for the removal of these things,
who deceive and murder Your sheep,
who verbally vomit on their peers, the young and the elderly,
who pounce on the elderly and helpless and unsuspecting children and
who think nothing will ever happen to them because they think
     You do not exist.

I pray that You show them Your light so they can find the path to You.
I pray that You soften their hearts so they can have feeling.
I pray that You remove the hard scales from their eyes so they can see
     clearly.

I was once lost; only by Your grace, my Father, am I now found.

Let them know that You do exist and that the trouble and grief they
     cause others will be defended by You.
Let them know that You are the deliverer of justice to the oppressed
     and although the deliverance may not be right this second, it is
     coming and they will have to face it.

However, Father, if they knowingly choose to continue in their wicked
ways, when Your justice reigns on them and when You have Your
vengeance please shield Your flock from having to witness it.

Although, at times, we may say we want to be the fly on the wall when
they get theirs or we can't wait to see them get theirs or just simply
hope for vengeance against our enemies,
     forgive us Father. We know not what we do.

**Lead us not into temptation, but deliver us from that evil way of
thinking so we may see Your Glorious face one sweet day.
In the name of our Lord and Savior Jesus Christ we pray! Amen!**

The steps of a *good* man are ordered by the Lord : and he delighteth in his way

Though he fall, he shall not be utterly cast down : for the Lord upholdeth *him with* his hand.

– Psalm 37:23-24 (KJV)

Repentance for failing God

Father, please forgive me for falling short of Your desire for me.

There have been times when I have wished for the gifts You bestowed upon others.   **But, I do this no more!**

I appreciate and am grateful for all of the gifts You have bestowed upon me, Father. Reveal them all to me, Father. I know now that what You have for me is for me and what You have for others are for them.

> No longer do I wish to be deceived, as Adam and
> Eve were when they were tricked into focusing on
> the one thing in Your beautiful garden they could
> not have, instead of keeping their focus on all the
> other things in Your garden they could have.

Please forgive me, Father! I recognize and accept the responsibility of this fault of mine. Even if I were deceived, I willingly walked in those feelings, and I truly wish to repent from that way of thinking from now on. I will focus on the gifts You have for me because they are the gifts given to me by You. I thank You for every one of them, Father.

In the name of Jesus, please forgive me
for failing You,
for not always being patient and understanding toward others,
for getting in the way of Your divine will for me,
for running away from You for so long,
for being disobedient and disrespectful to the Holy Spirit,
for not continuously giving forth a forgiving nature,
for not forgetting or letting go of past pains,
for breaking one of, therefore, all of your commandments.
for every sin I have ever committed.

Father, please place Your whole armor of protection around me, in the name of Jesus.

Please guide my thoughts, my heart, my actions and especially my tongue. Keep me from committing deliberate sins and from causing anyone else any form of pain, in the name of Jesus Christ I pray. Amen.

Repentance for failing God / Praise

Father, thank You for tolerating me when I am disobedient and fall short of Your will; Your ultimate plan for me.

Please forgive me for my shortcomings and for all of my sins. I do not intend to be disobedient, however, I make no excuses. I willingly repent right now, in the name of Jesus Christ.

Father, I also wish to thank You for continuing to love me when I am not so loveable. And, when I fall down, thank You for picking me up, Lord. I know there are many who have fallen before me and there may be others to fall after me. They may never be allowed to get back up again. Thank You for deeming me worthy of being picked up and to be chosen. Thank You, Father, for Your Grace and Your Mercy.

Without You, Father I am and could do nothing! Praise You in the name of Jesus Christ. Amen

<u>Repentance for placing others before God / Plea for guidance</u>

Father, please forgive me for breaking Your first commandment. I allowed others to come first in my life before You. No matter what I did to earn their affection, and I always felt I had to earn it from them, but they always placed others ahead of me.

> *Then one day You informed me I am one*
> *of Your angels and oft times angels are*
> *overlooked until they are needed.*

Father, I profess right here and right now that I much rather be Your angel than their flunky!

Thank You for straightening me out!!

Father, when I have felt unappreciated by others, thank You for acknowledging me and showing me that You appreciate me.
I know I am not supposed to look toward others. Please forgive me right now for succumbing to those feelings, in the name of Jesus Christ.
Father God, I just ask that You show me how to express love and give of myself without overdoing it to the point of feeling **unappreciated, hurt and overlooked, just to mention a few.**

I give so much of myself to others, but don't receive the same in return. And because I know I shouldn't look for reciprocity, I'm asking You to mold me into a person who will give without expectations and without overdoing it.
Mold me to be able to hold a door open for someone out of the kindness of my heart and not expect a thank You, even if it is a basic ethic.
Finally, Father, although I cannot receive a physical hug or kiss from You, which I find myself in need of at times, I know that You love me, unconditionally, no matter what. Thank You, Father for choosing me before I was a thought. Certainly, the evil one tried to get me, but You have shielded and covered me always. I am, indeed, grateful. Praise God forever and ever. These things I ask and I pray in Jesus' name. Amen.

Repentance for feelings of resentment and harsh anger

Father,   please   forgive   me   today   for   holding
on   to   feelings   of   resentment   and   anger.

**I felt like lashing out! Had it not been for You I know I would not
have been able to hold back.**

Father I don't want to continue having these feelings; I don't know
how to get rid of them. **Help me, Father!**
It feels like I don't have control when they are upon me. **Help me,
Father!**
At times, I can feel the adrenaline flowing and then a rage comes forth
before I can do anything about it. **Help me, Father!**
I am very afraid of what I will do when this happens because a feeling
of destruction comes over me. **Help me, Father!**

Father I need You to guide me away from this negative way!

When these feelings are upon me I bring about pain toward others
by stabbing them with a sharp tongue,
by verbally vomiting on them,
by causing them some sort of mental anguish. I even want to,
if not already done so, strike them with an angry hand or other
weapon.
I have even wished they were never here.

**Father, please forgive me and help me remove these negative
thoughts and feelings! I don't want to hurt anyone in any kind of
way anymore!
Father, please help me! It hurts to feel this way knowing I don't
want to be like this.
I am powerless, but You are almighty! I am weak, but You are
strong!**

Help me! Deliver me, Father!

In the name of Jesus Christ I pray. Amen.

I cry out to God Most High,
to God who will fulfill His
purpose for me.

He will send help from Heaven to
save me,
rescuing me from those who are
out to get me.
My God will send forth his
unfailing love and faithfulness.

-Psalm 57:2-3 (NLT)

Plea for change of heart

Lord Jesus, please guide my tongue and my thoughts.

> Give me the courage to look my enemy directly in the eye
> with a sincere smile; to love them as if they were
> You, Father.

Teach me to be the better person.
Teach me to get past **their** feelings of jealousy, envy and even hate
toward me, instead of harboring or developing ill feelings
toward them, and especially toward those who have caused
me any form of pain in the past or present.

Keep those demonic spirits from jumping into me.
Keep me from being as petty as they are.

Bind them back into the pits of hell where they belong, in the name of
Jesus Christ.

Indeed, the vengeance is Yours, Lord.

I pray that You have mercy on those who have caused me pain.
I pray that You touch their hearts and move them to make amends to
You for their shortcomings.
I believe by my praying for them You will also help me to forgive and
let go of the pain.

Keep me from allowing or inviting any stains to reside on my heart.

Continue to allow me to see and discern all of my enemies, yet move
me to respond toward them righteously.

Move me to do Your will at all times Father, in the name of Jesus
Christ.

I don't want to harbor any ill feelings anymore.
I don't want to have a hardened heart anymore.
I don't want to be the person I used to be anymore.

Your command is my wish. Please, be with me Jesus. Amen!

Plea for deliverance of hardening of the heart

Father, today I feel like it is me against not only the
worldly, but the whole world. Or, better yet, it seems
like the whole world is against me.

No one is in my corner and I am being taken for granted, so it seems.

I feel unappreciated and pushed aside, once again, by those who say
they love and appreciate me, and by those who say they know
and love You.

At times I feel my heart hardening or drying up toward them. As a
result, right now, I am fighting the urge to cry.

I don't want to feel this way, Lord.

Please deliver me from these feelings, Father, in the name of Jesus.

I come to the altar to leave these feelings here for You to dispose of as
You will.

Father, help me, guide me and keep me, Lord, from picking these
feelings back up again.

In the mighty, matchless name of Jesus Christ I pray. Amen.

Plea for deliverance of negative characteristics

Father I thank You for exposing some of the negative characteristics
that I, unfortunately, posses. Even though, at times, I don't
like what I see, thank You for showing them to me anyway.

Father I thank You for allowing me the opportunity to pray to You for
a cleansing and for a deliverance, while working toward
becoming a better person.

I don't want to hold on to the bad anymore.

Please free me of the anger and all feelings that hold me back and
weigh me down.   They are a direct deterrent to my positive
growth, progress and Your love.

I want to remain in my Heavenly Father's good Grace and in His favor.

Lord, please help me!

I don't want to be this way!

I want to leave these
angry,
enraging,
mean,
insensitive,
uncompromising,
uncompassionate feelings and all negative feelings on Your altar to be
discarded.

I don't want them back, either!

Most of all, I don't want to disappoint You, Father.

**I want to make You proud enough of me to continue to identify me
not only as Your daughter/son, but definitely as Your friend.**

Lead me in the name of Jesus Christ. Amen

<u>Let Go and Let God</u>

Inside I have wept monsoons of grief
　　　　because I followed the will
　　　　　　　　of myself and the thief
　　　　　　　　　　Why do those tears still come
　　　　　　if the pains are from the past?
　　　　I should be rid of them at last
　　　　　　FEAR NOT!!
They say upon their arrival—for those pains and tears will not last
　　　　　　He will send you a comforter
　　　　　Lift up thine eyes and see His Glory
　　　　Only those who knows what he knows
　　　　　　　　goes
　　　　　　that is no tall tale or story
　　　　　　　Who was it that said the sky is the sky,
　　　　　　　　　the ground is the ground
　　　　and what I hear indeed, is a sound?
　　And who said you are my trend setter?
Anything you can do I can do better!
Why are there stars and who says they are what they are?
　　Why is there a sun and a moon
　　　a May and a June?
　　　　　　　And what ever happened to the other 10?
　　　　　　　　　The stars may say yes,
　　　　　　　but I say they say no
　　　　　　And the sun won't shine until I say so
　　　　I can even tell you when the world will end
I th—I th—I think I can predict the future *my friend*!
　　　　　For so, so long my ears were blocked
　　　　　and my mouth was wide open
　　　　　exposing my stupidity trail
　　　　　I delved into the future
　　　　　　head first to no
　　　　　　　avail
　　　For so, so long I have remained in the past
　　　　Twirling down the drain of despair
　　　　Pointing and placing blame
　　　　　for the reasons I have
　　　　　　failed
　　　Oh, my Lord, my Savior, my Jesus
　　　　　Please hear my cry!
　　Help me salvage what is left of my PRESENT
　　　　before I die!

13

Plea for deliverance of sins   *Inspired by Psalms 19:12*

Our Father, who art in Heaven, Hallowed be thy name.
Lord, I don't know all of the sins I am capable of and I don't want to.
I do know that I want You to deliver me from them so I won't cause
     havoc on others.

Don't let those sins take control over me.

Deliver me from every hidden sin and character defect according to
     Your will.
Deliver me from committing any deliberate sins, Father.
Release me from every hidden evil spirit that is buried in me only to
     control and devour my soul.
They don't want me to inherit what they renounced. Yes, Father, there
     are those who believe and follow the will of the one who is
     here only to seek, kill and destroy throughout the land.
They have no remorse.
They care for no one.
They are selfish in all they do and in every way, except in their misery.
They desire to get me to join them in their misery.
          But they will soon fall harder and longer than the
     walls of Jericho.
They will be crushed like the Philistine's in the temple that once held
     Samson captive and they will forever drown like Pharaoh's
     army in the Red Sea; only it will be of fire.
Nothing of theirs will ever be found again.
There will be no skulls, bones or any remnants of their existence.
They are the enemy of the Sovereign God.

You will capture, seize and destroy them all, Father.

Father, I pray to You now asking for Your strength, Your wisdom and
     Your discernment to overcome their cunning, deceitful
     trickery.
I am not the wiser Father without You.
Without You, Father I may as well be one of them.

**With You, Father I can do all things as You choose to strengthen
me.**

Right now, I choose to be Your flunky Father.

Right now, I choose the same prayer of Jabez who asked, "Oh, that You would bless me and enlarge my lands! Please be with me in all that I do, and to keep me from all trouble and pain!" (1 Chronicles 4:9 NLT)   That is my prayer today, my Father.

I have faith.

I trust and believe in Your son, my Lord, my Savior and my big brother Jesus Christ, who decided to sacrifice His life for me.

Although I can never thank You enough, Father I thank You ever so much in the Precious name of Jesus Christ. Amen.

Plea for God's intervention from attacker *Inspired by Psalm 7 & 26*

Save me, God, as I come to You, the Sovereign One, to seek refuge
from my enemies.

I will continue to ask for Your help as I realize I need You more and
more every day.
I also realize I cannot live a righteous life on my own. I need You in
order to do that.
I need You to protect me from those who willingly choose to attack me
and wish to cause me any and every kind of pain.

Lord, please hear my humble plea for protection.
Save me by Your unchanging hand.

Test my thoughts, examine my heart and trace my steps. If You find
something amiss in any of these things, if You find that I am
not willing to change and refrain from sin, then let those
without pity track me down to have their way, Lord.

I know I am a sinner but I am not a persistent sinner.
If You find that I have followed Your commands so I would not
surround myself or embrace myself in the midst of cruel and
evil people,
if my steps have stayed on Your path and I have not willingly wavered,
if I have honored the faithful followers of the Lord and have kept their
promises even when it hurts,
if I have not broken my vows to You even when it hurts,
if I have refused to accept bribes to testify against the innocent,
if I despise those who are persistent sinners,
if I have refused to slander or speak evil of friends and others,
if I have spoken the truth with a sincere heart,
if I have not deliberately caused harm to my neighbor and have led a
life to do what is right, then guard me, protect me and
consider
me a friend of God.
Stand against those who do the opposite. Judge them as only You can.
What is most important, is that You have Your way Lord.

Indeed, no weapons formed against the children of God shall prosper.
In the dominant name of Jesus Christ I pray! Amen.

Plea for God's intervention from persecutor

Father, I know that You are aware I need You right now. I know because You have just guided my tongue and directed my thoughts while I was angry just now.

What was meant for evil, You changed to good.

Thank You for keeping me away from the evil of causing someone else harm or pain.

Father, I need You right now as I am currently being persecuted and I feel like lashing back at them.
Father, please help me get rid of the anger and don't allow me to become resentful or hold a grudge against them.

For some reason I am holding on to it and I don't want it at all!

Help me!
Guide me.
Direct me away from spewing these feelings and demonic spirits on anyone else.

Father I place these feelings at the altar for You to dispose of in the sea of forgetfulness.

Deliver me from all negative characteristics that would keep me out of Your will, Father.

Please keep Your whole armor of protection around me, Father, and I pray that You touch the heart and mind of my persecutor, altering their negative ways toward being more righteous.

In the name of Jesus Christ, I pray! Amen.

<u>Plea for God's Intervention from evildoers</u>   *Inspired by Psalms 10*

Father, at times is seems like You are so far away from me. It is as if You have removed the light of Your lighthouse from shining on me.

And because of this it also seems as though the evil and the wicked are able to prosper in all they do, especially and most emphatically in persecuting me.

Lord, I know You are not far away from me.
Lord, I know You will punish the wicked.

I know You haven't forgotten me because I trust in You, Lord.

I trust that You see the pain and grief the evildoers cause and that You will deal with them in Your time.

Vengeance is Yours, Father.

I just ask that You give me the wisdom to know when to get out of Your way, the patience to wait and let Your will be done, the strength to hold on and the courage to stand firm.

It is not harm that I wish for these evildoers, Father. It is a change.

But I know it is not my will that will take place. It is Your will.

Therefore, let Your will be done in the name of Jesus Christ! Amen!

Plea for God's Intervention from feelings of emptiness

Lord, I feel as though I am so alone right now.
I feel like I am at the bottom of a long list and the best is not saved for last; it is at the top.

Lord, help me get past these feelings.

Please fill this void, this emptiness in my heart.

I am not capable of doing this on my own.
I realize that I need You more and more each day.
I was a fool before I met You, thinking I was in control of my life.

Right now, I wish to refrain from those foolish ways and cast them and every demonic spirit, with their evil owner, back into the pits of hell where they belong, in the name of Jesus. I plead the blood of Jesus on them and by Your word Father no weapons formed against me shall prosper. In the name of Jesus I pray. Amen.

<u>**Plea for Guidance**</u>   *Inspired by Ephesians 6:12 - 20*

Father, I don't want to repel people from me, however, I don't invite
the enemy to come at all.

> Your word says, *"For we wrestle not against flesh
> and blood, but against principalities, against powers,
> against the rulers of the darkness of this world,
> against spiritual wickedness in high places."*
> *(Ephesians 6:12 KJV)*

Guide my thoughts and my tongue immediately, Father, so I will not
destroy or damage my soul by following those wicked powers
with retaliation or by responding toward them improperly.
Yet, grant me boldness that I may speak as I should, making known the
mystery of the gospel.

Indeed, daily I must take on the whole armor of God because I am His
soldier and I am on the battlefield fighting for the Lord!

My armor consists of the breastplate of righteousness. My feet are
shod with the preparation of the gospel of peace;
both are to stand and to withstand the evil that walks to and
fro daily seeking to kill and destroy.
I wear the shield of faith to repel the darts of the wicked, the helmet of
salvation, the sword of the Spirit, the Word of God!
I plead the priceless, precious blood of Jesus Christ on everything
wicked!
I bind and rebuke them all back into the pits of hell where they all
belong in the Paramount name of Jesus Christ!!

Bless His Holy name!! Amen

Plea for Guidance to deal with other believers of the Gospel

Father I am standing in the need of a blessing, right now, Lord.
I am in need of strength and wisdom in coping with the trying times I
am currently experiencing.

In particular, Father, bless me with more patience, compassion, love,
      warmth and understanding for my brothers and sisters in
      Christ, who are critical of or lack understanding of my
      relationship with You.
Anoint my senses to comprehend how to show them compassion and to
      continue to treat them lovingly instead of with contempt.
Show me how to deal with them lovingly if they emit a spirit
      contradictory to Yours.
Keep me from resorting to jaded ways when trying to communicate
      with them.
Teach me patience in dealing with them and lead me to pray for them.
      In the matchless name of Jesus Christ I pray! Amen.

Just Lead Me

Lord, for those who do not understand
or who have not been touched by Your
unchanging hand—lead me, Lord. Just lead me.

When I speak of the things You have done
especially of the victories with You I have won—
lead me, Lord. Just lead me.

Some don't want to hear what I have to say
so I ask of You to show them in Your own way
and always—lead me, Lord. Just lead me.

They claim to be one of your own
I don't want a sinful judging seed sown
so, I ask You — lead me, Lord. Just lead me.

I always want Your guidance, love and protection
along with Your Grace, Mercy and affection
please—lead me, Lord. Just lead me.

Plea for Strength in the midst of Fear *Inspired by 2 Chronicles 20*

Lord, lead me to do as Jehoshaphat did when he faced an army head on.
Many today would have felt compelled to run and hide while others would have felt compelled to fight and die.

But Jehoshaphat did neither.

Instead, he sought You out, first and foremost, for guidance and
    direction.
As a leader he led his people to seek not himself, not his mightiest
    warrior or soldier, but You Lord.

Indeed, he was a good leader by example and not by mandate.

Although I am not a leader such as Jehoshaphat, I want to follow in this
    example of his in every decision that I must make.
I will seek You for my decisions, as did Jehoshaphat.
All that I ask is that You bless me with the serenity
        and the courage not to run and hide,
        guide me with the wisdom not to fight and die,
        and the strength to stand firm in the midst of all fearful things.
And always, move me when I am in Your way.

In the mighty, mighty name of Jesus Christ I pray! Amen.

Plea to Strengthen Friendships

Father I have come to realize that friendships are synonymous to
marriages. Even though they are intimate relationships
between two people that are not sexual, they are relationships
that develop when two people get together and learn each
others ways.

Guide _____ and me in our friendship with each other, Lord, as
You guide us in our friendship with You.

Guide us not to judge or base old damaged friendships on our current
friendships.

Please remove any jealousy, envy and past hurts and angers.

Strengthen our spiritual union with each other as we become
strengthened in You, Father.

And if we are not meant to be friends then separate us, Father. In the
name of Jesus Christ I pray. Amen.

Plea for Protection

Lord I have many persecutors. Some are for reasons unknown and some are for reason I have no control over.

Lord please, be a protective shield around me daily so they will not be able to prevail against me, one You have claimed as Your own.

Let these enemies lay a trap for themselves for they are unGodly, as You bless the Godly by surrounding them with Your shield of love. Yes, Lord! End the wickedness of the unGodly, but help all those who obey You in their hearts and minds.

The unGodly are cunning as they will only confess with their mouths, yet not with their hearts or actions.

Today I proclaim that I confess with my mouth,
as well as with my heart.
And I say let my actions speak louder than my words.

I will thank the Lord because He is Holy, just and pure.

My Lord, my Savior I will lift Your name on high.

Praise the Sovereign God of us all!

Plea for God's Revelation of Self   *Inspired by Jeremiah 33:3*

Father, in the name of Jesus,
please reveal to me
what You will have me
to know on this day.

Reveal the mystery
of Your will for me
on this day, Lord.

And when reading Your word,
Father, reveal to me the mysteries
of Your word, in the name of Jesus.

Please guide me
and direct me
to carry out Your will
on this day.

Use me Lord
for Your will
and Your will alone.

Where there is trouble,
sorrow,
lack of understanding,
lack of guidance
or just a need for someone to vent with;
wherever I can assist,
use me, Father
to carry out Your will.
And still, cover me with Your whole armor of protection
against every evil presence.

**I plead the blood of Jesus upon them all and bind them back into
the pits of hell where they belong! In the mighty name of Jesus!**

Douse me with your anointing my Heavenly Father.
Give me courage to withstand all that comes against me in carrying out
Your will, wisdom to know when to get out of Your way,
serenity to accept the will You have decided and
strength to endure to the end.
In the magnificent name of Jesus Christ I pray. Amen.

Plea for Self Revelation   *Inspired by Psalms 7*

Father, in the name of Jesus I ask that You reveal to me who I am.

No matter how much I don't like what I see about myself, no matter
how ugly it is, show me so that I may know what to pray to
You to change in me.

Father, show me when I have done any wrong or injustice to anyone,
when I have betrayed a loved one or friend,
when I have attacked an enemy without probable cause; most
emphatically, show me when I have sinned against Your way.

Whenever it is my wrongdoing Father, show me and allow me the
opportunity to make amends to You and/or to whomever.
Allow me the chance to repent and restore the spots I have
placed on my heart, so my name will be clear in Your book of life.

If it is not my wrongdoing
please inflate my heart with Your divine love so I will not hold a
grudge, hold on to the pain or remain angry with whomever about
whatever.
Allow me to show them love.
Allow me to keep the focus on myself.

I don't want to cause them pain.

And Father, as I move forward, please guide my thoughts daily to
coincide with Your thoughts.
Guide my tongue daily to coincide with what You want me to say.
Guide all of me daily, Father to do Your will, Your way in the
matchless name of Jesus Christ. Amen

Plea for Clarity of Enemy

My Heavenly Father, please hear my plea. You have revealed to me there is an enemy in my midst.

P l e a s e   m a k e   i t   m o r e   c l e a r   t o   m e .

For some reason I am blinded or hindered from seeing who is being used by the enemy.

Father, I need to see and I need to know exactly whom my enemy is
        using to try to destroy me.
Father, no matter whom it is, I need to know because they are contradicting Your will, which is now my way.

Then give me the courage, the strength and the wisdom to deal with them as You so choose.

Father, please open my eyes so I may see who they are.
                Open my ears so I may hear them coming.
Touch my heart so I may deal with them righteously.

        In the untouchable name of Jesus Christ I pray. Amen

Plea for Strength/Courage to deal with an enemy

Father, in the name of Jesus, please help me deal with this cunning,
evil, demonic spirit that is using the flesh of one who smiles in my face
and who others don't seem to recognize or want to acknowledge.
Indeed, it is crafty. It waits until no one else is around or
it disguises its mess with humor,
fooling the others.

Father, please continue to bless me with the discerning ability to know
when I am dealing with the spirit of the enemy,

yet
give me the wisdom and the strength to handle both,
the wicked spirit and the flesh that embraces the
wicked spirit, according to Your will and Your way.
Righteously.   In the name of Jesus.

And, guide me to keep Your loving spirit so I won't direct toward
those in Your flock what should be directed toward the serpent.

Most emphatically, Father, place in my heart the spirit to love even my
worst enemy, the strength, guidance and courage
to put the evil spirit in its place, without
causing harm to the flesh being
used by the evil spirit.

Even if said flesh desires and embraces such larceny in their heart,
guide **me** righteously, Lord.
Continue to make **me** the better person.
Allow **me** to keep the focus on **my actions** and **not theirs**.
Keep **me** from reacting unrighteously.

I ask in the priceless name of Jesus Christ I pray. Amen.

Hold On

When the vessel from whence we have come has gone away
Although it is hard, do not stray
For Jesus is the only way

Don't lose his divine, undying connection
Ask the Lord for Aaron's peace and for God's whole armor of
protection

It may seem like your nucleus or reason for being is gone
Just remember God's unchanging hand and just hold on

Jesus Christ is the one we look to and lean on—it is a must
The Lord is our shepherd, in Him we must trust

So, don't ever think that you are in this world all alone
God is with you forever, to embrace you with the love He has always
shown

One For The Family

Last night I laid down and wept
    well before I slept
On other nights when I would cry
    until this day I didn't know why

Jesus, my Lord, please help my prayer get through
    another force is trying to keep me away from You
Lord, with You is where I want to stay
    they are always tempting me to go astray

But their talk is foul like the stench from an opened grave
    one knows they are unGodly, simply by the way they behave
Indeed, they are drowning in deep waters unseen by the naked eye
    waters I once embraced; that kept me and mine from touching
the sky

That is why
    on others nights I would cry

See, I was totally blind and I could not see
        Huh, but I thank God my mother prayed for me
And, although she is no longer here physically
        I still hear my momma praying for me

As a result, my blindness is being lifted
        but other families are still being sifted
Into a wide lake of despair
        led to believe there is no one who cares

But **GOD**, in all **His** wonder
        will let no man put asunder

We bind every evil spirit!
WE BIND EVERY EVIL SPIRIT! to hell
        and must do all we can
            for the family we must make a stand
                and reach for the Precious Lord's hand

Mothers, you are the strength and the glue
        that is why I am begging you
Take back your husbands, daughters and your sons
        from the grasps of the evil ones

Your family is being sought simply for destruction and
        ultimately to be killed
            To drown in those deep waters where the thief and
            his imps are willed

If it had not been for the Lord on my side
        and my mother praying for me
Only our Heavenly Father knows where
        in the world I would be

Plea for Strength in Home Going of loved one

Heavenly Father, every time I have come to You for
refuge You have kept me safe.
I know coming to You now for a healing You will provide it, indeed.

Father I need You to help me cope with the home going of my loved
one. I miss them greatly.

I want them to be physically here with me. Please forgive me for being
in this selfish mood, Lord.

Although I know my loved one is in a wicked less, painless place and I
am to rejoice at their going home to You,
I am finding myself missing
their touch,
their kiss,
their sound,
their hug,
their voice,
their physically being here with me.

For right now, just looking at a picture is not enough.

When I think of the times together with my loved one,
it only makes me miss them that much more.

At night I hide my tears in my pillow and
I cover my sadness with a false smile during
the day because I don't want a pity party or
anyone's sorrow. I just want my loved one back!

As I said, I am missing my loved one greatly.

Please, help me cope today, Father!

I know this too, shall pass, but it is too difficult to do on my own.
I need You, Lord, to help me get through.

In the name of Jesus Christ I pray.

Plea for Strength to stay on the Righteous Path

Father, I hate and despise all wicked things!

Bless me with the ability to discern when I am in the presence of
iniquity.
My heart desires to be away from all who willingly and/or knowingly
cause harm or pain to others.
I do not wish to be around them at any time, unless it is Your will to
use me in order to bring them closer to You.
And, if that ever is the case Father, please give me strength, courage,
love, patience, compassion and understanding to carry out Your will.

Otherwise, I have no desire to be in their midst or environment.
They are the enemies of my God, my Father.
I have no desire to embrace my Father's enemy, who is my enemy.

It is my desire to endure the fullness of my Father's splendor,
to walk on His streets of gold,
to see loved ones who have made it there before me.

These are just a few of the reasons why I will walk on the righteous
path to victory and glory, with the help of my Heavenly
Father.
I will continue to praise the Holy, Paramount God and continue to bless
the name of my Savior, Jesus Christ.
I will change my thoughts and my will to the will of God.
I willingly give God my all on His altar of sacrifice.
I am His clay to be molded and moved as He will have me.

My faith and trust remain in Him, who saves and protects me on a daily
basis, and loves me like no other ever has or ever will.

He has loved me well before I was even thought of.

Indeed, I love the Lord! He heard my cry and answered me before I
was through asking.

Thank my Heavenly Father for Jesus, who redeemed my wretched
soul! Hallelujah!! Amen

The Light of the World

Why are you always so critical of the things I do?
Especially since I try, very hard at times, just to please you.

Toward you I'm developing a hardened heart
Lord knows I don't want that to take part
I wish I had been different from the start

But I wasn't so now I must change
My whole attitude, I must rearrange

Whoever doesn't like it that is their problem
I'm not going to try to solve them

If they don't like it, too bad! They can scratch themselves and get glad
No longer am I walking around being sad. Now, I'm mad!

Not necessarily at anyone else
Primarily and most definitely at myself

Sometimes I feel like a jackass
And it feels like I get there so fast

without asking for directions
and far away from corrections

I have often asked the Lord, "Why me?
Why am I the one always treated so harshly?"
Lord said, "Do you remember what happened to me

on my way and while I was on the cross?
Keep this in mind daughter/son, it is their loss

You must continue to show kindness
to their hardened blindness

You must continue to show them love
as I do you from Heaven above

You must not allow them to send you back
to the time when your heart was black

Continue to love them all
so you won't be included in the fall

However, if there is a snake in your face
you must put it in its place
otherwise they will win this race

I know it will be a very difficult task, indeed. But I am sure
you must be the stronger to last, so these things you must endure"

Garment Words

I cry alone only at night
      because I don't want a pity party
That is when no one else is in sight
      I don't want them around then, not hardly

So why, why, why must I cry and suffer?
While others smile and are born with either
      a solid or plated silver spoon
Because, because, because you have asked to be
      like your big Brother . . . and that silver . . .
      will turn to rust very soon

My Father's comforting words helped restore
      my withering soul
      like the woman who touched the hem
I am unlike a wingless bird, indeed, I am not
      half. I am made whole.
      No longer to worry about them

Plea for Strength in weakness

Father I want for me what You want for me; because now, I see.

Now I understand why I am to endure longsuffering.

Now I understand why trials and storms are to come in my life.

Now I know You want me to be a soldier who will
not waver during these times of distress.

I believe You want me to be a warrior
who will stand in the presence of turmoil,
who will not falter in the presence of the enemy
nor fear them.

I believe You want me to be a warrior who
will not give up or give in.

I believe You want me to endure the testing fires to become that solid
piece of gold, molded only by You.

I believe You chose me to be with You in eternal bliss
when Your final judgement has become manifest.

Because of these things I ask You, Father,
wherever I am weak
please make me strong.

In the Priceless name of Jesus Christ, I pray, Amen.

Plea for Strength not to retaliate

Father my heart is heavily burdened right now.

I am in deep distress.   I am hurting so right now.
        I feel like lashing out at those who have hurt me.

Some of them may be wheat, while others may be tares; I cannot tell the difference.

But nevertheless, I feel like lashing out at them. However, I don't want to because I know that is not of You. I know it would be unrighteous of me.

Father, please, I am placing these feelings on the altar for You to remove from me and place them into the sea of forgetfulness, never again to return.

I do not wish to be as harmful, nor as hurtful to them or others as they have been to me. Father, please help me be the better person no matter how hard it is, in the name of Jesus Christ.

Give me the strength not to allow the things evildoers say to affect me or cause me to react and act negatively, in the name of Jesus Christ.

Help me understand that I am not wrestling with the human being before me, but realize when it is the spiritual wickedness that is coming against me because I am Your child, Father, in the name of Jesus Christ.
And please have mercy on the human who enjoys and embraces such wickedness, for they know not what they do. Reveal to them the pain they cause and allow them the chance to repent, in the name of Jesus Christ.

If they chose not to repent, then let Your will be done, Father. I ask these things in the mighty, matchless name of my Lord and my Savior Jesus Christ. Amen.

Plea for Strength to Hold On/Praise

Father, everything I have belongs to You.

I have everything because of You. Praise You for choosing me to endure trials and tribulations.

I know they come to make me strong.

Praise You for choosing me to endure persecution.

I know a great reward awaits me in Heaven.

I just ask that You give me the strength to hold on to Your unchanging hand.
Give me the courage and the wisdom to know when to stand and when to move.

In the loveable, paramount name of Jesus Christ. Amen.

Don't worry about the wicked.
Don't envy those who do wrong.

For like grass, they soon fade away.
Like springtime flowers, they soon wither.

Trust in the Lord and do good.
Then you will live safely in the land and prosper.

Take delight in the Lord,
and He will give you your heart's desires.

Commit everything you do to the Lord.
Trust Him, and He will help you.

– Psalm 37:1-5 (NLT)

The Lord saves the Godly;
He is their fortress in times of trouble.

The Lord helps them,
rescuing them from the wicked.
He saves them,
and they find shelter in Him

– Psalm 37:39-40 (NLT)

<u>Plea for Cleansing of the Heart/Praise</u>   *Inspired by Psalm 20*

Father You know the desires of my heart.

Whatever desires that are not of Your will or that are not becoming of
    You at all, please cleanse me from them right now and
    forever, Lord.
Erase them all from my memory; wipe them away from all of my
    senses.

All I want to do is please and praise You, Lord.

**I know that whatever Your will is for me,
You will make a way.**

I thank You for it right now, Lord. Even though it hasn't manifested
    itself in my life, yet.
I thank You right here and right now in the name of Jesus.
I thank You, who gave and continues to give His all to me, one You do
    not need.
I thank You, who continues to be patient with me and my
imperfections,
You, who heard me when I cried,
You, who holds me when I stumble,
You, who are with me even when I falter,
You, who allow me to endure and experience the trials and tribulations
    that come to strengthen me,
You, who acknowledge and appreciate me when others don't or won't,
You, who told the angel to watch over me as I slept last night and told
    the angel to wake me this morning when You didn't have to,
You, who loves me just as I am,
You, who will not let go of me,
You, who chose me out of the faces of many.

I thank You Lord! I Praise You!

And in the words of Jehoshaphat's singers who sang to the Lord,

" . . . I give thanks to You Lord. His faithful love endures forever!"
(2 Chronicles 20:21 NLT)

Plea for Rescue/Praise

My Master, please deliver me from all who hate me.
Give me victory over my accusers.
Hold me safely beyond their reach.
Block me from their vision.

It seems as though they are coming at me with both barrels and I have no way to escape the harm they have directed toward me.

Father and friend of Abraham. I walk with You as my Father and my Friend. In doing so, my enemies become Your enemies; they have no where to run or hide with You by my side.

Thank You for showing me what unfailing love is!

Once I began to learn and follow Your laws
I have been blessed with a revived soul,
I have grown wiser,
I have a constant Joy in my heart and
I have used the gifts and natural talents You decided to give to me.

Thank You for blessing me ever since the day I accepted my Lord and my Savior Jesus Christ.
As a result, You have accepted me in Your
anointed, sacred flock.

Thank You in the name of Jesus for choosing me.

And always, Father God, may my actions,
the words from my mouth
and the thoughts from
my inner soul please
and praise You at
all times!

In the Blessed name of Jesus Christ I pray. Amen.

Praise/Plea for strength

Father, now I understand why I should count it all joy
when facing trials and tribulations, because what
You have just allowed me to come through,
indeed, has made me the stronger.

How so wrong I was to believe I was weak the other way around, when
I would **react** to certain individuals or particular events or happenings.

How so wrong I was when I used to sulk and have pity parties with
myself.

How so wrong I was not to purge away those pains.

How so wrong I was to hold on to those hurts and sorrows.

How so unappreciative and ungrateful it was of me to wonder why
those trials and tribulations were happening to me.

I was blind then.
But, now, I see!

Thank You for every trial and for every tribulation!

I count it all joy!

You have guided me to a higher level of handling the trials and
tribulations that come my way.

Thank You for loving me enough to have me endure them all. And for
those to come, I thank You in the name of Jesus.

Even though, at times, they may be difficult and they may be hard to
bear, I know that not only are You always with me, but You will also
always see me through.

I know that You will always make a way for me.

So Father, thank You for removing the sadness that haunted me from
the past and thank You for replacing it with joy.

41

Father, I must ask in order that I may receive.

In my every weakness please make me strong.

Lead me so I can come home to spend
my eternity with You Father.

In the precious, untouchable name of Jesus.

Do not envy others-
it only leads to harm.

Count It All Joy

A particular green
is the meanest I've ever seen

Now, hear this! Now, hear this!
The paper version is not the worst,
but the love of this
will cause all
to fall
into a destructive abyss

In case you didn't know, this green, while on its course
is driven by a steady, negative force

whose only will
is to seek, destroy and kill

When it is directed toward you
don't get mad
be glad
in fact, have a Beatitude

It's Not the Color

I don't always like green
It is the most resentful I have ever seen

It fills me with pain, even today
And it is difficult to clear its stains away

The hardening of the heart
Toward the one who took part

Indeed, I don't want that to remain

<u>Lymerically Speaking</u>

The most resentful thing I have ever seen
and associated with so much pain is green

The love of it is the root of all evil
it destroys bonds between loving people

It allows negatives to come in between

...My heart is confident in You, O God;
no wonder I can sing your praises!...

– Psalm 57:7 (NLT)

Praise Him

Father, Praise You for this lovely day!
Praise You for keeping me from evil today!
Praise You for keeping me from causing pain to another!

I delight in feeling Your love.
I delight in experiencing Your mercy and Your grace.

> The pleasure is mine as I am more than willing
> to be Your lump of clay.

> I am ready, willing and desire You to mold me into
> the likeness of Your desire.

> Praise You for touching me this morning and
> for placing this smile upon my face.

Although there are things going on in my life right now to make me
angry, upset, mad and sad, they just don't equate or come close to the
things in my life that I am joyous about, namely You, Father.

Praise You for all of the natural gifts You have showered me with.
Praise You for the wonderful people You have placed in this
new life You have given me.
Praise You for giving me this new life.

> Thank You for showing me such a good time; I thought it
> would be boring on Your side of the fence.

> Thank You for proving me so wrong! It is much
> more exciting, warm, loving, peaceful and abundant!

Praise God! Amen!

<u>Praise for Blessings</u>

God has blessed me with so many things.

He sent His only child, His Holy Spirit, love, peace, Grace and Mercy.

From now on I just want to do God's will.

I have been tithing and it is coming back to me more abundantly.

In obeying my Father, He blesses me with constant joy!

It would be foolish to turn away from Him..

I always want to stay in my Heavenly Father's good
Grace and in His favor.

In the name of Jesus Christ, I praise You! Amen.

Praise for Deliverance/Godly love

Father, thank You for showing me how to trust and how to love again.
I had lost faith and hope in life in general until You came to
set me free from depression, insecurity, shame and despair, among
other things.

Before then, I thought I had no reason or purpose to live. However,
once I experienced Your divine love, it was reason enough to
want to live.

To do what pleases You is what I now strive for.

I am bothered just by the thought of disappointing You, all because
You have shown me love when I didn't even love myself.

It definitely makes a difference knowing, for sure, that I am loved by
someone. Thank You for loving me Father, in the name of
Jesus.

Now I am learning to love myself.
I am learning how much You really love me.
It is a love unlike any other.
It is, most emphatically, far greater than any other.

There are no words that would fully describe or completely express
how very grateful I am for Your love, mercy and grace!

I don't know why You deemed me worthy, but I question it no longer.
From now on I accept it, appreciate it and I cherish it for the
rest of my days.

Thank You for choosing me, Father.

In the matchless name of Jesus Christ, Your beloved, firstborn and only
begotten Son, I pray. Hallelujah! Amen!

Praise for Deliverance from shame and depression

Father You alone pulled me out of deep, dark, murky waters.
I was succumbed by darkness and saw no light.

Slowly,
ever so slowly
my soul, my spirit
my whole life was drifting
away from where it belonged.

Now I can say that I'm so glad for the day Your love lifted me!

I'm so glad that Jesus loves me and yes, I love the Lord!

He heard my cry!

He gave me an immediate response
when I called out to Him, my Savior.

Bless His Holy Name! Hallelujah!
Praise God Almighty for sending
Jesus to save my whole life.

Thank You, Jesus!

You are my redeemer, my Lord and my Savior because You sacrificed
Yourself for me.
You are my Counselor because You guide and direct
my path perfectly, which makes You worthy to be praised as my King.

You are my Rock, my Strength, my Fortress and my Protector because
You keep me and protect me from harm and danger.

You allow no weapons formed against me to prosper.
You not only warn me of the enemy, but You also place Your shield of
protection around me daily.
You are my Confidant and my Best Friend
because You allow me to give You all of my troubles.
You allow me to come to You at all times, no matter the time or day.

You are always available
to me and I always have Your undivided attention.

You are always there and You will never go away.

I know that the only way I will lose You is if I walk away.

I have been there and don't want to ever go back.

You encourage me instead of putting me down.

You love me unconditionally.

These are some of the reasons
why You are my Master and my Everything.

Praise the Lord! Hallelujah! Amen!

Poetic praise for Deliverance

Heavenly Father, thank You for the deliverance from depression!
Thank You for showing me Your glorious light when I was twirling
     down a draining depression!
Thank You for delivering me from the iniquity nestled in my heart!

In a prayer I told You I didn't want to be that way; I didn't want to
     hold on to those negative feelings anymore.

I believed You would deliver me.   You delivered me!
You set me free!

Thank You my Heavenly Father. Praise You!
     Let my life always praise You!

Hallelujah, Amen
Hallelujah, Amen
He's done a wonderful thing for me
When he set my heart free
Hallelujah, Amen

Hallelujah, Amen
Hallelujah, Amen
He's done a wonderful thing for me
When he gave my mind peace
Hallelujah, Amen

Hallelujah, Amen
Hallelujah, Amen
He's done a wonderful thing for me
Now my spirit is at ease
Hallelujah, Amen

Hallelujah, Amen
Hallelujah, Amen
He's done a wonderful thing for me
For Him my soul will please
Hallelujah, Amen

Praise for Rewarding Obedience to the Lord

My Precious Lord and Savior Jesus Christ, thank You so much for keeping Your word.

Thank You for not failing me.
Thank You for not abandoning me.
Thank You for loving me before I loved You or myself.

When I asked to walk with You on the water You allowed me to do so with open arms.   When I began to sink I kept my focus on You, instead of the water.
              I was desperate to get out, but You told me to wait.

I remembered, in Your word, when You told Your friend Abraham to sacrifice his beloved son Isaac, You knew Your friend's heart was heavily burdened.   You knew he didn't want
                          to carry out Your will.
I can only try to imagine that this burden was unmatched by any other he had ever experienced at that time, yet he still set out to do as You had instructed.   He was obedient to Your word.

Abraham's reward was another ram in the bush in the place of his beloved son Isaac.   **Praise God!!**

Father, You knew I did not want to wait when You told me to. But I was obedient to Your word.
              I waited as You instructed me to and You rewarded me.
You held my hand and led me out of the water safely!

Without You I would have struggled, causing myself to drown in murky, sinful waters.
        With You I was rewarded with another ram in the bush.

Praise God Almighty, the Beginning and the End, the Alpha and the
        Omega, the Paramount, Sovereign Father for being all
              knowing, all seeing, all mighty and all powerful.

Thank You just for being You! Amen! Glory to God!!

Praise for Spiritual Gifts to Deal with co-workers/bosses

Thank You for blessing me with more patience, compassion, love,
warmth and understanding for the co-worker(s)/boss(es)
I deal with on a daily basis who are negative,
uncompassionate,
unfeeling
and evil spirited.

It was easy for me to show warm feelings toward the positive ones,
but not for the other.

I needed Your help so I called out to You to guide me and grant me
those gifts to deal with them.

As always, You came to my rescue!

You opened my eyes to those who meant to cause me harm.

You were the force behind me treating them with kindness!

Thank You for changing me!

Thank You for showing me how to deal with them
lovingly instead of with malice or anger.

Thank You for showing me how to deal with them firmly, yet without
being as nasty to those who were nasty toward me.

As a part of my upbringing, You placed me with those who taught me
to be real with and true to myself.

As a result, I can be real with and true to these co-workers/ bosses
who have a spirit contradictory to Yours.

Thank You for filling my heart with love and understanding
so I would not resort to their same slithering ways
when they try to damage my credibility.

Thank You for teaching me patience in dealing with them, knowing

full well they were trying to destroy me by bearing false witness
toward my work ethics and against me in general.

Thank You for revealing to me that the job is all they have.

Yet, in You, I am blessed with so much more.

Thank You for leading me to pray for them instead of sinking in their
quicksand of anger, jealousy, insecurity and hate
that leads to so much negativity.

For, indeed, misery loves company.

Thank You for teaching me and for continuing to teach and guide me
toward a better way of living.

Your lessons have taught me how You are faithful
to those faithful to You.

You give Yourself to me as I give myself to You;
You give so much more than that.

You also continue to show me unconditional love.

You know all there is to know about me
and You still love me.
All of me.

Regardless of my imperfections.
You still love me.
Unconditionally.

You have proven there is no greater love!

I love and praise You Lord! Praise You in the name of Jesus Christ.

Amen.

Praise for Spiritual Gifts   *Inspired by Psalms 18*

Lord, I love You!
>You warned me of the coming of my enemies.
>>You let me know I had Your protection then and I
>>have it always.

Thank You for the gift of discernment!

I did not know this was a gift from You, but I graciously accept.
>Please continue to bless me with this gift, any and all others
>You wish to send my way.
>Please continue to protect me with Your impenetrable shield
>of love, mercy and grace, in the name of Jesus!

Not only did You save me, You also strengthened me by Your
response.

>Like when the people questioned Moses' authority,
>You responded. When they disobeyed the order You
>delivered through Moses, again, You responded.
>You will always protect Your anointed and You will
>always respond when Your anointed is disturbed in
>any way.   Thank You for choosing me, Lord!

Thank You! Praise You for taking on all of my battles!

Please forgive me when I get in Your way.
>In fact, please reveal it to me when I am in Your way
so I can move with a swiftness.

>Praise You for assuming all the vengeance
so I won't bring damnation upon my very soul.

>Thank You
for taking care of those who come against me. In essence, they don't
realize they are against You as well.

Your example is what I try to follow by asking our Heavenly Father to
forgive them . For they know not what they do.

56

No Weapons

Not one of us has any earthly idea of all You are capable of.
We have no way of conceiving or comprehending all that You
are. However,

I do know that You are all powerful and all knowing.
I am forever grateful that You are all that You are and You
saw fit to chose me as one of Your own.

There is nothing that I could do that would come close to fully
thanking You for all You have done for me.
Even if I said Thank You, non stop,
for a trillion years, it still wouldn't be enough or even come close to all
that You have done, are currently doing and will do for me.

Thank You for hearing and answering my disparaging cry.
Thank You for all of the blessings, all You have done, all currently
being made manifest in my life and all You have for me in the future!

And, Father, thank You for blessing me with
another privileged day to carry out Your will,
another privileged day for Your usage, AND
another privileged day of learning the lessons You have
designed specifically for me.

I thank You for shining Your Heavenly light upon me.

Praise the Holy, Heavenly Father in the name of Jesus!

Praise for warnings

Lord, I thank You for warning me whenever trouble is near.

If not for Your warnings, where, oh where would I be.

I would be less than the dust under the shoes of my enemies.

Thank You, Father for loving me as You do.
Thank You for showing me Mercy and Grace.
Thank You for loving and caring for me before and greater than any
        other living soul, including myself. I don't ever want to know
        life without You again, Father.

                    I love the life I have with You! Therefore, losing
                    You would be losing life!

All the glory and praises to You, my loveable and Heavenly Father!

      I Praise You! I love You! I exalt You, my Heavenly Father!
                Hallelujah!!! Amen!

Praise for Saving me   *Inspired by Footprints*

As I think about some of my past experiences, Father, I see the times
        death stared me dead in the face and I didn't even realize it
        was happening or that You were right there.

        Now I know that You were there and You saved me on every
            one of those occasions in my life.

Then I didn't recognize You. Yet You still saw me through and
        protected me from those certain harms,
            those certain dangers,
                those certain deaths.

Indeed, there were numerous times when I could have lost my life
without knowing You.

Like the song says,

> *I am a living testimony*
> *I could have been dead on gone*
> *But, Lord You let me live on!*
> *I thank the Lord that I'm still alive!*

Thank You for keeping me!
Thank You for walking with me during all those times, Lord.
Thank You for carrying me when I didn't have the strength to walk on
my own.
Thank You for allowing me the opportunity to make amends to those
who I have caused pain.
Thank You for blessing me with the courage to make amends even
when I am not at fault.

Lord, thank You for the lesson You taught me
about the power of saying I'm sorry without
a but at the end to nullify the apology.

Most emphatically, Lord! I know had it not been for You, then and
        now, I would have been a lost soul fallen from Your grace
        forever.

Thank You, Father, for loving me.

Thank You Jesus for redeeming me and for being my strength, my rock, my fortress, my Savior, my shield and my intercessor.

Praise the Word of God and praise our Heavenly Father, who I love.
Praise God, my Father for saving my life.
I   a m   s o   g l a d   Y o u   h e a r d   m y   c r y !

He chose me; He could have overlooked me, but He chose me.
He died for me; He could have stayed in Heaven, but He died for me.
He cleansed me; He could have left me dirty, but He cleansed me.
He changed me; He could have left me the same, but He changed me.
He healed me; He could have left me broken, but he Healed me.
He took the pain of sickness away from my loved one by leading them
     home with Him.
He allowed me and said loved one to bloom and heal into a better
     relationship well before calling them home.
He gives me peace.
He protects me.
He walks with me and He talks with me.
He has told me on more than one occasion that I am His own.
He told me, my Father told me that He is my mother; He is my
     everything, indeed!
He loves me and He comforts me.

My Heavenly Father is so good to me.

God is the one and only true love of my life!

As a result of knowing His love, I can give it to others.

All the glory to God for changing my heart!

Thank You God for allowing Jesus Christ to mend my bond with You!

You are the well of water in my soul!

Praise You always and forever!

Amen!

Praise for God's Intervention/Plea to continue

> *Father, please forgive me today. I had long feelings*
> *of resentment and some anger today. I felt like*
> *lashing out, but I know it was You who held me back.*

Thank You for sending one of Your many angels to help me today.
        Just their presence was enough to soothe me and their listening
                to me vent was very comforting.

Father, thank You for Your patience in dealing with me.

Thank You for allowing my departed loved one to comfort me spiritually.

Thank You for not only hearing my cries, but also for answering my prayers.

Thank You for stopping me from lashing out.

Thank You for correcting my negative thoughts today.

Thank You for showing me those thoughts would have caused pain to another.

Thank You for allowing me to shed and purge away pain.

Please continue to direct me on that path, Father.

In the name of Jesus Christ I pray.

Amen.

Praise for God's Protection   *Inspired by Psalm 18 & 37*

When I was drowning in deep waters of despair,
Lord,
You reached down from Heaven into those murky waters and rescued
me.

When I was down, in my weakest moment, my enemies kicked me,
knocked me down and stood on top of me,
Lord,
You led me to safety.

These were my rewards for doing what was right; for not turning away
from God.

Because I am not wicked You haven't shown me hostility.
Because I am humble You have not humiliated me.

You have rescued me and humiliated the proud.
You have brought me out of darkness into Your glorious light.

Thank You, Lord for being my shield of protection during every storm
that has come my way. Thank You, Lord for being my solid rock of
security when I was not secure with myself.

Thank You, Lord for the strength and security that You provide me
with Your open, loving arms. Thank You, Lord for reaching for me
when I didn't know how to reach for You.

Thank You, Lord for loving me totally, completely and unconditionally
like no other has or ever will. Thank You, Lord for holding my hand
when I stumble; restraining me from falling.

> Your loving, supportive, secure hands make me surefooted
> and steady on any terrain.

Thank You, Lord for showing Yourself faithful to me as I have been
faithful to You. Thank You, Lord for showing integrity to me as I have
shown integrity to You.

Thank You, Lord for showing yourself pure to me as I have been pure
to You. Thank You for doing all these things for me even when I don't

always do these things for You.

Thank You, Lord for removing the stains away from my heart. Thank You, Lord for giving me the victory.

Thank You, Lord for showing unfailing love to me. Thank You, Lord for taking on my worries.

Thank You, Lord for fighting all of my battles. Thank You, Lord for keeping me away from feelings of envy.

Thank You, Lord for destroying the wicked. Thank You, Lord for taking care of me.

Thank You, Lord for allowing me to live in prosperous security. Thank You, Lord for severing the hold of the wicked.

Thank You, Lord for allowing me to fill my heart with Your will and Your way. Thank You, Lord for not forsaking me.

Thank You, Lord for coming by here. Thank You, Lord for redeeming me and buying me with Your priceless blood.

Thank You, Lord for saving my whole life. Thank You, Lord for Your gentleness and for Your love.

Thank You, Lord for all You have done for me. Thank You, Father for not feeling as though the priceless blood of the lamb would be wasted on saving me.

I praise Your Holy name.

I sing Hallelujah and all glory to God on high!

Holy, Holy, Holy is our Heavenly Father!

Praise for God's unfailing love

My Lord, my Savior I trust in Your unfailing love.

     Because You have rescued me from the clutches of my enemies I can lift up my hands to praise You freely and come to You rejoicing and lifting Your name on high.

Lord, You have been so good to me, even when I wasn't good to myself and even when I was disrespectful to You.

Hallelujah!!

I sing praises to You, Lord!

You have loved me when no one else loved me, including myself and You have never ceased.
You have never left me;
You have always been there for me even when I just knew of You.

Now that I have finally turned from the world and returned the loving embrace, to You, who has been there all the time just waiting and desiring to be in my life, I have a joy in my heart that I never had before and never want to be without again.

I have a certain peace in my daily walks with You, Lord.
I have indeed, found a certain kind of love now that I have found You!
I have faith knowing You will never take these feelings away from me.

These things I have found since I have stopped running away from You.
I would lose everything by walking away from You.

Thank You for loving me when I didn't even love myself!
Thank You for loving me so much that You shed Your own blood for me and that You took it upon Yourself to experience the most painful death for me.
Thank You, Father for loving me so much that You sacrificed Your only begotten son, Your one and only born child, for me!

Praise You in the name of Jesus Christ.

Praise for God's Mercy and Grace

Heavenly Father, I thank You for having mercy on me. You saw how I
    suffered at the hands of those who hated me without cause and
    You rescued me from their poisonous fangs.

As a result I was able to rejoice and praise Your name, indeed, without
shame.

You told me not to be ashamed of You otherwise, face Your being
ashamed of me.

I thank You, Lord with all of my heart.
I will testify of the miracles You have performed in my life.

Today, I have unspeakable joy all because of You.

I praise Your Holy name Jesus.

You alone were my shelter when I was in the midst of the storms of
life.
You were my refuge during all of the trying times in my life.

And, because I trust and have faith in You, You have never abandoned
me. You have always been right by my side.

My Lord, You have always kept me. You have never let me down.
And when I walked in darkness, You walked with me.

Praise You, Lord! Never again do I want to live another day without
You in my life.

A mere moment out of the palm of Your unchanging hand
will seem like days,
those days will seem like years
and those years will seem like an eternity.
Without You I may as well be one of the walking dead.

I thank You so much, Father because but for Your Grace, go I.

Thank You for having mercy on me and for choosing me to be watched
by the mighty,
untouchable,
infallible,
perfect,
loving,
caring shepherd, Father.

I am so grateful my Heavenly Father is the
all knowing,
all mighty,
merciful,
omnipotent,
omnipresent,
Sovereign God, and that You are that You are!!

Indeed, You and only You are worthy to be praised.

Blessed be the Holy Father, who allows the sweet, Holy Spirit to rain
down on me.

Thank You, Father for all You have done for me.

> Glory, glory Hallelujah! Glory, glory! Hallelujah! His truth is
> marching on!

Praise for Rescuing me

Lord You are
my strength,
my rock,
my fortress,
my savior.

I desire to remain ensconced in the palm of Your loving, unchanging hand.

It is my desire because:
when I was weak, You helped me stand.
When I was tired and worn, You helped me through the storms.
When my spirit was dying, You restored and strengthened my soul.

Lord, I love You!

When the world's noose tightened around my neck,
when I was sinking in the flood of destruction,
when death looked me straight in the eye,
I cried out to my God for help.

He not only heard, He also answered my cry.

Vengeance was and is His and His alone.

He is my fortress during the times life sends battles my way.
He is my shelter during the storms that life sends my way.
He is my strength when I am at my wits end, weakest point and cannot defend myself.

His love for me is more solid than any rock, jewel, gem or stone ever found or that ever will be found!

The Lord Jesus, He is my Savior!

Savior, sweet Savior! Thank You for not passing me by!

Please continue

to revive my soul,
to cleanse me from hidden sins and evil spirits of my past and
to keep me from deliberate sins.

Guide my thoughts toward You.
Guide my tongue to speak Your words and order my steps toward Your
righteous path to do the will of
Our Father who art in Heaven.

In the name of Jesus Christ I ask all these things. Amen.

Praise for Restoring Faith

Lord I thank You for reviving my soul.
>There have been numerous times when I felt as though I was drowning in dark waters.
And just as I was about to go under, You reached down with Your
>almighty hand and pulled me out.

>Please forgive me for ever doubting Your existence.

I am forever grateful and
You are more than forever worthy to be praised!

Thank You, Father for restoring my faith.

Thank You for allowing me to get back up again!

No other love is even a distant second to Yours as Your love is indeed,
unlike any other.

I truly thank You for loving me so much that You would endure all that
>You have endured just for me.

What a wonderful God You are!

What a loving and merciful God You are!

What an awesome God I serve!

Praise You, Heavenly Father.

In the name of Jesus Christ.

Praise for being the Sacrificial Lamb

Lord, thank You for dying for me. And before You died for me, Lord
thank You for being
scorned,
      mocked,
           deceived,
                criticized,
                    beaten,
                        stabbed,
                            tortured,
                                tested,
                            challenged,
                      thought less off,
                looked over,
            ignored,
        forgotten,
     ridiculed,
laughed at,
      deserted,
          kicked,
             slapped,
                 punched,
                     spat upon,
                         crucified,
                              lied on,
                         talked about,
                    slandered,
                mistreated,
             scandalized,
          abused,
misunderstood,
         hated,
             envied,
                doubted,
                     tormented and
                            unappreciated,
             among other things, just for me.

Had it not been for You, Lord, I know I would be rotting flesh right
        now, with a forever tormented spirit.
But because You chose to be the sacrificial lamb in the bush, I can live
a life filled with
        peace and abundance,
                love and joy, and the
                        trials and tribulations to make me strong.

I can live knowing that I have the victory.

                    Thank You for showing me the light.

Thank You for not failing me even though, at times, I fail You.

          Praise God almighty!

        In the only, all powerful name of Jesus Christ!

Praise for Another Day

Father, thank You for allowing Your angel to watch over me last night as I slept.

Once more, I am grateful You have allowed Your angel to touch me
this morning, in the name of Jesus Christ, allowing me the
privilege to serve You just another day;
to carry out Your will, Father.

In the name of Jesus Christ, I thank You
for Your Grace, for Your Mercy and for
Your divine, precious, ubiquitous, undying, matchless love!

Praise for Strength

When I walked through the valley of the shadow of death,
thank You for walking with me, Lord.

I was comforted knowing that You were with me.

I was not afraid.

You are the Master carpenter, who molds me according to the will of
our Heavenly Father.

Although it is trying for me at times, I trust in You Father, because I
know that You are all knowing, all seeing, all Powerful and
You will not lead me astray.

**I have blessed assurance that You will see me through whatever!
Whenever!**

You have blessed me with gifts my enemy doesn't understand and
those which I never knew I was lacking, like unconditional
love and patience.

You have restored my spiritual soul when it was hanging down like a
weeping willow tree.

Now I have an everlasting Joy and a peace in my heart knowing that
You are leading me righteously, in the name of Jesus Christ.

**I hunger for the Holy Spirit;
for Your anointing oil.**

Praise You, Father. Indeed, You are Sovereign!

Be exalted, O God, above the
highest heavens.
May Your glory shine over all the
earth.

– Psalm 57:5 & 11 (NLT)